Hallowed

Hallowed

Patricia Fargnoli

New and Selected Poems

Tupelo Press

North Adams, Massachusetts

Library of Congress Cataloging-in-Publication Data
Names: Fargnoli, Patricia, author.
Title: Hallowed : new and selected poems / Patricia Fargnoli.
Description: First edition. | North Adams, Massachusetts : Tupelo Press, [2017] |
Includes bibliographical references.
Identifiers: LCCN 2017026600 | ISBN 9781946482006 (pbk. original : alk. paper)
Classification: LCC PS3556.A7144 A6 2017 | DDC 811/.54--dc23

Cover and text designed and composed in URW Baskerville by Bill Kuch.
Cover and title page photograph: "Beech Leaf in Snow" by John Lehet (www.lehet.com).
Used with permission of the artist. All rights reserved.

First edition: September 2017.

Poems in this collection have previously appeared, in some instances in different versions,
in the books *Necessary Light* (Utah State University Press, 1999), *Duties of the Spirit*
(Tupelo Press, 2005), *Then, Something* (Tupelo Press, 2009), and *Winter* (Hobblebush
Books, 2013).

Tupelo Press
P.O. Box 1767, North Adams, Massachusetts 01247
(413) 664–9611 / editor@tupelopress.org / www.tupelopress.org

Tupelo Press is an award-winning independent literary press that publishes fine fiction,
nonfiction, and poetry in books that are a joy to hold as well as read. Tupelo Press is a
registered 501(c)(3) nonprofit organization, and we rely on public support to carry out
our mission of publishing extraordinary work that may be outside the realm of the large
commercial publishers. Financial donations are welcome and are tax deductible.

ART WORKS.
arts.gov

Supported in part by an award from
the National Endowment for the Arts.

To my family with love,
and in memory of Roger Jones

Contents

Hallowed: New Poems (2013–2016)

from Necessary Light (1999)

from **Duties of the Spirit** (2005)

from **Then, Something** (2009)

from **Winter (2013)**

Hallowed: New Poems (2013–2016)

To an Old Woman Standing in October Light

Better to just admit it, time has gotten away from you, and yet
here you are again, out in your yard at sunset, a golden light draping itself

across the white houses and mowed lawns.
The house-tall maple, green and rust in ordinary light,

has become a golden leaf-embossed globe, the brook runs molten,
the clouds themselves glow gold as the heaven you used to imagine.

Do you know that your own figure, as Midas-touched as a Klimt painting,
has become part of that landscape falling around you,

almost indistinguishable from the whole of it —
as if eternity itself were being absorbed into your mortal body?

Or is it that your body, out of time, is merged into eternity?
You have been looking for a reason for your continued existence,

with faith so shaky it vibrates like a plucked wire.
Such moments of glory must be enough. As you search them out again, again,

your disappearing holds off for a while. But see how, even in this present,
as you stand there, the past flies into the future,

the way, above you, the crows are winging home again, calling to each other,
vanishing above the trees into the night-gathering sky.

The Hours

I. Lauds

Three a.m., I wake out of darkness into darkness,
all is quiet, outside no one moving, the apartment windows dark,
the pole lamp the only light but light enough to cast
a shimmer on the web woven across my window.
A restless night with many awakenings. But I rise
praising life for continuing, praising the automatic
coffee pot and the stillness into which I move
slowly as my body unarches itself, my feet grow
more stable beneath me. I rise with my thoughts
on the day which itself is rising out of the night
as gradually as the opening of the morning glory.
I would say to the departing night, you have given me
wakefulness and you have given me sleep and dream
and I am not who I was any longer.
I would say to the arriving day, come with all
your tasks and appointments, come with all your uncertainties,
and I will travel through you knowing by nightfall
I will no longer be who I am here in this quiet dark hour.

II. Prime

*". . . et opera manuum nostrarum dirige super nos et opus manuum
nostrarum dirige"*

Seven a.m., Lord, as I move out of darkness and deep shadow
that has just broken through into the sunlight
that washes the rhododendron, border trees and the facades
of these apartment buildings with gold-green light.
I have risen early and so now am moving past the four hours
since sleep into thoughts of what needs be done today.
I have written in the journal, I have made lists of tasks:
to cook the shrimp and spinach recipe from the internet,
to answer the e-mail from my grandson who asks
how many poems he needs to publish them,
and to let in the Housing Authority people for the inspection.
I have only to write this poem. Hardly anything —
for this quiet day and rest, I am grateful.

But this, too, is my work for the day:
let all that I do be in kindness and with the thought of others
for whom the day will be a struggle to live. The refugees,
by the hundreds of thousands who seek a home.
And the many living with war, with houses turned to rubble,
with explosions in the marketplaces, with thirst and hunger.
Here are my prayers for safety of those and of my grand-nephew
serving in Dubai, who served also before in Iraq and Iran,
whose mind is wounded by the trauma he's seen.
I hold so many people in my heart, spirit, you whom I call Lord —
because I believe that somewhere, in some form, there exists
an eternal Intelligence who may or may not know me. This hope is my help.
I lift my voice to it — my voice, joyful and praising, my voice trembling
with fear for the world, this prayer of first daylight, this long oh of sorrow.

III. Terce

Let the five lilies in my garden burst open their tight buds.
Give me the comfort of my cat's paw against my cheek,
let the UPS man arrive with the new microwave
as I have been days without one
and let the maintenance man come to fix the leaking freezer.
Let my afternoon nap be long and the pillow soft.
Let the spider in the corner of the portico protect her egg sac.
Let the skunk stay hidden until evening
and a red-tail lift up high in a sky like blue crystal.
Give me energy to go for my walk by the brook even though
it is only rock-bed and cracked mud in these days of little rain.
Let my neighbor walk beside me with her golden poodle
or let me walk alone to take in the wildflowers on the bank.
Give me stronger legs and breath that comes more easily
as if it might come from my very soul.
Give me certain knowledge of the soul, Lord,
since my doubt is my deepest sadness.
Is it held within my body or does it hover in the ether?
Will it continue after, and what will it be like then?
Will I remember my sons and daughters, my poems?
Please let me remember them.
Soul which is like a brook flowing with pure water,
soul which opens like lilies under the sun,
soul as hidden as the skunk in daylight,
as free as the red-tail circling, circling,
soul that knows the language of the weaving spider,
and of the fables my cat speaks in my ears
and the many names of the wildflowers and wild grasses.

IV. Sext

Today, at this high hour, the clock's hands move together like lovers
until they seem to be one.

The sun is invisible behind the milky-gray sheet of clouds
which are releasing rain,

soft rain dotting the puddles stretched glossy and thin
along the black sidewalk.

I keep returning to sleep in the hope I will sleep deeply enough
to erase the pain.

Let the rain come down all day and ease the discomfort, Lord,
if you are anywhere.

Let me remind myself that this hour is the hour of the crucifixion
when the sky darkened.

Let me remember also that it is the hour of highest light, where across
the world millions kneel down.

Let me remember the rain will cease and the sun will burn down
again from the heavens

where it resides among universes of suns, suns dying, suns being born,
beyond even scientists' imaginations.

I have become old. A long time, Lord, since I have felt the joys I used to feel.
Bring back those feelings again

as when I went out into the noon fields of autumn gathering bouquets
   of dried weeds,
or when I sat long before the ocean

as if watching a play about the creation of the Earth, as the sun gold-plated
the surface of the moving waters.

V. None

Mid-afternoon — an early autumn hour

when the sun begins to lower in the chill blue sky,

throwing a slanted light across the landscape, sharpening the edges

of the buildings, deepening the colors of the fields and foliage,

those leaves starting their slide into brilliance, into death.

Sometimes I nearly believe that answers to all my doubts

and questions might emerge from such a light.

VI. Vespers

Bless this hour in which the sun has lowered leaving only
the alpenglow in the west
and the lanterns outside the apartments which have turned on automatically,

the ones on the black wrought-iron poles and the ones on the buildings,
throwing off a rose-gold flush
across the sidewalks and lawn so that the daylight is replaced —

one sort of light switched out for another, and all around
a hush settling in
as if dusk had smothered all sound, the birds' last calls as they head home,

the last cars pulling in to the parking places, the last lawn chair folded
against the walls of the porticos,
voices stilled to whispers: *bye now, see you later* as the residents close their doors.

This is the hour for giving thanks and so I do, counting up the blessings
of this day in which nothing special happened,
unless I count the absence of illness, the companionship of my cat.

Unless I count a sense of peace and quiet and rest. I am grateful
for the poem that came from my hand
and the poem that hasn't come but will come another day.

I am grateful for the friend who lugged away many boxes of books
because when I move, I cannot take them all. And for my children
and grandchildren and great-grandchildren one hundred miles away.

Bless dusk with its blue shadows, bless the holy singing of the autumn cicadas.
Bless these cool nights
and warm days, and the fox that will come in the night hunting.

Bless the spiders weaving webs and laying egg sacs on my portico walls —
their legacy. Bless dusk, again and again,
magician who, under his dark cloak, makes the world disappear.

VII. Compline

These early winter nights,
I go to bed early.
And the old childhood prayer
comes back again — *now I lay me down.*
Let the pressures of this day pull back
the way the outgoing tides draw
the green waters back from the shores,
leaving where they were,
only the hard-packed sand
below tideline, strewn with bits of shell,
a few strands of kelp,
the detritus of the day.
This has been a day long in hours,
slow in the passing of time
because I have done only a little:
made meals I've eaten alone,
read poems, written a poem, napped.
Whatever I have done today
that does not live up to my desire
for perfection, forgive.
Whatever I have not done today
to stand up against the brutalities,
forgive.
I am tired — my years as heavy on me
as the house-sized boulders on the forest floor.
Lay me down.
May sleep come quickly and be unbroken.
May a silence fall over my body
the way snow falls on a pond.

Dabhne

I

Once, as she walked home from school,
a child was pursued into the woods
by three boys who wanted perhaps
to trap her, perhaps just to scare her.
But the child knew what to do, in her mind
she had rehearsed such an occasion
and she kept walking, ignoring them.
When they didn't leave, she hid
behind trees, scrunched down in undergrowth.
The boys crossed the brook on the stones.

> *Somewhere in Europe*
> *an artist has carved a young beauty*
> *into the trunk of a laurel.*
> *She is looking down,*
> *curls around her shoulders,*
> *her face as sad as rain.*
> *A robe is wrapped tightly around her.*
> *Ivy has climbed up over her body.*

The boys gave up at last and went home.

> *Her father, the river god, has saved her*
> *from Apollo who, full of lust,*
> *had been chasing her through the forest*
> *and had almost overtaken her.*

II

I don't know if there were three boys, but there were some,
and there was a brook.

III

Or begin again:

It was the first day of first grade. After school let out,
some big girls chased me in the woods that bordered
the parking lot. They left me alone there in a clearing.

No wind, no birds, no sound. The towering nightmare trees.
In a panic, I ran like a whirlwind first here, then there, searching
for a path.

> *When Daphne became a laurel, the other trees gossiped,*
> *the messages traveling through their root systems,*
> *some saying she ought to have given in,*
> *he was a god after all; but some praised her.*

My father had walked partway
to the school and was waiting for me in the half-dark.
Where were you? he said, when I found my way out.

> *But Daphne, you remember, was never released;*
> *her skin remained bark, her hair, leaves,*
> *her arms, branches.g*

A Fable

the woman pulls on her robe of orange

      and goes to sit by the sea

all day the dizzy gulls float above her

        give me they say

your orange heart

I will she says   and gives them her heart

      above her the clouds   are whining

they say they are dry   give me

they say

your tears   willingly the woman

gives them her tears   and the rain falls on her

now says the ocean   I have need

of your life

     but the woman in the robe of orange says

at last

     no you cannot have my life

and she gets up and goes away

in her flaming robe

taking with her

her striped umbrella

a pouch of green figs

her double-pawed orange cat

everything she has left

The Koi Pond

It was my house.
No, I don't have a house,
though I can imagine it.
It was my daughter's house
when the black bear came that summer,
with the red tags in her ears
and her adolescent cub beside her
and sat down by the koi pond
as if she was curious about those gold
and red and black streaks traveling
through the water, under the lily pads,
around the rocks.

You would have thought
she was hungry and would go after
the fish but she must have only
been entranced by them
because she didn't wade into the pond,
though she could have.
She only came quietly with her cub
and sat there for a long time watching
while the Ghost Koi, the Butterfly Koi,
the dark Goshiki and the Bekko
swam unknowing, undisturbed.

Who knows what was on her mind
because she came many times that summer
but never again, and I heard on the news
that three towns away, a bear
with red tags had followed a hiker
on a trail through a forest,
had come close and nipped at her shin.
I don't think the bear would have done
any real harm, but because of that

they captured her
and, this is oh so sad, killed her.

A bear's territory covers fifty miles at least,
so that must be our bear,
the one with the red tags in its ears,
the one my daughter told me about so I loved too,
the one she watched all summer.

Eastern Dobsonfly

Mid-July, my arms laden with groceries,
I am struggling to open the screen door when I see him:
five inches of fly if you count his antennae,
which cross over each other like a pair of sickles.
He doesn't move when I open the door,
doesn't move when I bend close to examine
the veined four-inch wings,
their gray latticed lacework folded along
his body, his beastly head, the mandibles
made not for eating but for
clutching the female.
I learn he has come from the nearby brook,
and has lived in all three worlds —
water, earth, air —
three years in water as larva
for which we have many names:
hellgrammite, crawlerbottom, go-devil,
then three weeks as pupa on land hidden under rocks,
until his last transubstantiation here so briefly in the air.
He has no need to eat, only to find a mate
and clutch her and multiply.
Corydalus Cornutes Linnaeus named him —
"noun meaning a form of bogey or a haunting spirit."
This is the second year
such a creature has alit on my door
same month of the year, in exactly the same spot.
He has only three days to live.
I will wear his likeness in a necklace of silver.

Dream Sequence

The Lover Returns

You make plans to meet in that Indian restaurant with the flocked
red wallpaper. You share all the old memories. He leaves. You know
he won't be there the next night but you go back anyway. Hoping. The
cashier at the restaurant tells you he called to say he wouldn't be
coming. Well, you think, he called. That's something at least.

The Vacation

You meet an elderly couple who invite you on vacation with them by
the sea in Maine. The cottage they rent is decrepit, and on the rickety
screen porch are two huge bees and a moth that looks like a biplane.
There is a space between the outside stairs and the door. You are afraid
to cross it.

The Way Is Hard

You are with your ex-husband at a crowded restaurant where you've
been given a corner table. No waitress comes. You decide to go to
the ocean. The waves are rough and wild and you are in danger of
drowning. It's winter, the walks covered with snow and ice. Nothing
is easy.

Pussy Willows

Some tiger lilies in a vase are dying of neglect. You water them and
they turn into pussy willows. You spray the room with Raid to kill the
bee, and close the door.

The Three Little Kittens

They are in the bedroom closet and keep getting out. Black, orange, white.
So cute. You can't keep them.

The Strange Pets

There is a barn behind your house where you keep your pet animals: a
combination moose/horse/cat and a feral creature, small like a weasel. You are
responsible for feeding them and giving them water. As the days go by, you
forget, so the animals become very weak and could die. You remember
in time.

The Web

An orb spider has built an enormous intricate web across the shed of your
childhood. It has taken many years to build and you want it to stay there.
Even the terrible landlord has put up a sign not to break the web. But a friend
comes and tears it down. You will never be friends again.

Needing Directions

You are driving to a workshop in a distant city but don't have good directions.
You are trying to find the street names on the map. All the names have to do
with dying: Mortality Way, Funeral Road, etc.

The Lobster Bugs

The landlord is inspecting your apartment. He opens the storage closet
to find it full of swarming bugs that look like lobsters. They get loose and
overrun the apartment. You wish you could have kept the kittens.

The House Cleaner

In the dream, you have a new house cleaner. She doesn't ask what to do
or how, but just starts in cleaning the living room, which is cluttered and
dusty. She thinks of places to put things and uses for them that you never
thought of.

Hard Balls

Your way is blocked by enormous red and black balls lying around the
floor. They look like bowling balls except they are bigger.

The Stolen Pocketbook

You are in a vast mall shopping for Christmas. Your pocketbook is stolen
six times by young toughs. You have no IDs or money. The police will do
nothing. This is the sixth time you've dreamt about a stolen pocketbook.

Ants

In the dream, there is an invasion of ants. You are feeling alone, lost,
incompetent.

Kios

You see "kios, kios, kios" written on a sheet of paper. You wonder if it
means "chaos" in some extraordinary language.

The Long White Plumes of Foam

In the dream, images of animals or people you have helped flash by, one
by one. None of the images has a background. Each image has a long
white plume of foam coming from or perhaps surrounding it. This is a
good dream.

Dead Woman Sitting

"Funeral poses mimic life . . ."
—New York Times, June 22, 2014

And so why not? Who wants to take death
lying down anyway? I mean to put some fun

in this funeral. I'll welcome mourners sitting up —
in a lawn chair, a chaise so I can stretch out tired legs.

A can of diet cola beside me, caffeinated for once,
a slice of that lemon cake from Shaw's

and a pack of Kent Lights so I can experience
again the pleasure of drawing in and letting go

the cloud rising beyond me into the ether
like so much dust. Dress me in jeans or my white linen

slacks and that J. Jill brown linen blouse I love,

the Indian earrings I bought at the side
of the Navajo trail one spring in Arizona.

And sandals, because they won't hurt my feet anymore.
Dear friends and family: wouldn't you rather

see me in my natural state instead of peering
down at me from the great height of the living?

Wouldn't it make you happier to know that, even after death,
I could be up and about — well not "about" exactly but up, at least?

I would no longer have any need
for my twenty pocketbooks or four winter coats in the closet.

See how death becomes me.
Wellness a permanent condition now.

Zugari

The combers breaking and breaking on white sand,
sand made even whiter by the Guadeloupe moon,

how, with nothing to hide them, the stars blanketed the sky.
We knelt at tideline while Zugari pointed out

the little fishes shoaling beneath the pier lights.
Without knowing each other's language

he explained to me with gestures that he wanted me
to come with him up the slope to his room in the help's quarters.

We climbed the path through the bushes though it was too dark
to see — but he took my hand to guide me.

It seemed right, the tree frogs saying so, the stars saying so,
his urging on my arm, the urging of my own body.

And when we made love in his plain white stucco room filled
with Mallorcan folk music from his radio, it seemed right and perfect,

the muscles of his arms hard under my hands, the muscles
of his chest lifting and falling against my body,

to be held as if fastened to each moment as it passed
into the next without a thought of the man left behind in the harsh winter,

of how short a time we'd have together, a week only, of his other women
from the weeks before, or the women who would come after.

Winter Day in New York City, 1973

Just divorced, a crazy year, everyone sleeping with everyone,
friends becoming lovers and back again, all of us filled with need.

That's the way it was when Marty and I, in my Karmann Ghia,
drove down to New York City from Hartford.

Washington Square strangely hushed that January afternoon,
stunned quiet by the harsh cold, the weight of gray sky.

Marty played chess with a local on a stone table as I shivered
beside him for what seemed like hours.

Snow started to fall, millions of pieces of glitter
through which we drove uptown until he found the bar

from the movie he'd seen. There he wandered away from me
into the crowd to try his luck with the city women.

Later on a side street, I changed into disco clothes in the car
while a doorman walked in circles in front of an apartment building.

Under purple strobes — a club named Wednesdays —
we danced together and apart until we were steamy and breathless.

When the place closed, Marty swiped one of their black balloons.
It floated us to Second Avenue where he tried to tell a homeless lady

how to find the Second Avenue bus, though at 2:00 a.m. there were no buses.
Back then, it seemed like magic, snowflakes lit by building lights,

Marty in his beard and Russian greatcoat, his arm sheltering my shoulder,
as we rushed downtown, uptown, the buzz and sparkle in the zero city air.

I drove us home as dawn was rising over skyscrapers and along the highways.
Marty slept. The radio played something I've long forgotten.

After Kansuke Yamamoto, from *Anxious Corridor* (1935)

One deer in the near-distance   a clearing beyond
the pillars of fir trees   deer and trees in silhouette but
                              around the deer the glow
of the sun so that the deer herself seems
                              to be lit up with a holiness
out there in that distance   which appears unreachable

                    To be truthful I can't see
what is anxious here unless it is   the creature herself
who has been made so visible
                              that any rifle could find her out.

Thus, it is
              as if she stands exposed at the boundary
between her life and her own death

though she may not be aware of it at all   or aware of the light
which surrounds her.

I want to step forward through the frame   to walk through
the high trunks of that dark forest

and approach her   not with death on my mind,
but with the desire for protection.   Oh vulnerable

                    deer of my own spirit.

Fragmenting

And the morning opens like a blue glory blossom on a vine.
The business conversations of the birds,
chitterings among the low bushes.

I want to be like the depths
beyond the petals where everything is burning.

The song I need to make it through today
falls on my head softly like the smallest pebbles

and keeps me from reaching out in sorrow.

Therefore I sing along and choose
among the many notes.

❦

All night, dreams came to rest in quiet,
unfolding into a kind of truth.
They shaped who I am.

The night nurtured them with its stars
as I turned to the wall.

❦

Later rain begins.

I feel the floor trembling
and the circle beneath my feet.

Inheritance and genealogy
on the curb talking

and the rain disappears into puddles.
I want to drift off to sleep

but I resist.
Then it floats me into its arms.

❧

Reality shifts like a hundred
golden fish shimmering in a net,

fragments that cannot be put together.

I cannot take it in — bigger than the mind
can keep at once.

What can it mean? I mean everything.
The lake at twilight, the lightning,
all the machinery around me?

❧

Once broken, things remain broken.
Words keep walking across the page
and a covey of doves scatters up.

I can never be close enough to the earth —
its vulnerable body, its almost silent heart,
so many souls riding on it.

❧

Some days I am all habits and compulsions
and then comes the sweet relief.

What if there is no choice?
Who is listening then?

All is vision and sound:
roar of garbage compactors in the complex,

clatter of hours, the hammers of morning,
the women rising, the women sewing.

Who hears voices when no one is there?
Do you even hear me?

Water in the River

Go down to a riverbank
Go where boulders grow by the water
Water whose surface reflects color and light
Water whose underside swirls in eddies and currents
Currents hurrying toward a big river
Currents moving downstream toward the sea
Sea calm and sea roaring
Sea full of mystery
Mystery of shallows and depths
Mystery of ships and shells
Shells containing life, containing absence
Shells smooth as pearl or broken
Broken ships on the floor of the sea
Broken lives there
There in the sea the river finds itself
There the jagged shells consume the ocean
Ocean full of the water of all rivers
Ocean full of rain and rolling
Rolling waves under an extravagance of clouds
Rolling cumulus hovering over water and land
Land that was born of the sea
Land that was volcano pushing up in fire
Fire born out of Earth's deepest places
Fire throwing lava and steam into the air
Air where no one is watching
Air of destiny and imagination
Imagination the place the mind makes
Imagination the water dancer
Dancer on the platforms of dusk
Dancer pirouetting across a wake
Wake of moon across water
Wake the ferry makes crossing the sound
Sound of horn enlarged in the fog

Sound of warning
Warning that darkness waits to come down
Warning rising over the islands
Islands that long ago rose from the sea
Islands of night where the people are asleep
A sleep of dreams as if risen from nothing
A sleep where nothing and everything is true
True are the great blue gray greens of the ocean
True are the rainbowed surfaces of rivers
Rivers come around again here to make a world
Rivers shining on a late August morning
Morning
World

Penitent Magdalene, Donatello

I

There must have been the rustle of tourists,
the lecture of the guide, but all I remember
is silence and the scent of antiquity all around me,
as if the statue and I were alone in the gallery
of Museo del Opera del Duomo on that Monday
when the tour bus was merely passing through for half a day,
when no other museums were open because it was Monday.
I remember her as small-boned, small in body,
though now I learn she is six feet tall.
I was stunned by love for her,
a sudden awakening into the pain of her —
her gaunt bony face, her fixed tortured eyes,
that held, in spite of that pain,
a glimmer of hope, of exaltation.

II

She was old by then in Donatello's imagination,
when he found the white poplar
and lifted the gouge, the chisel,
the carving knife to bring her
out of history into life again.
It must have been after Jesus cast out
the seven demons from her mind
and body, after she watched him crucified,
after the angels came to her in the empty cave,
after he, himself, appeared to her,
and after her years in the desert —
years of penitence and self-abnegation,
her wasted body, her uncombed tangled hair
reaching over her rags almost to her feet.

III

And yet, somehow she seemed beyond grief,
beyond suffering, her body, the dark wood,
gilded so that it held both light
and shadow, not beautiful, but beautiful
in her humanness. And as I stood transfixed,
in the center of the gallery,
where she stood on her flat stone pedestal,
encircled by the metal railing that kept me
at once close and distant, she imprinted me
with her mystery, she threw some bond
like a rope across the small space between us
and yes art can do this
so that now, decades later, she remains
bound to me, a presence in my body.

A Week after His Funeral

Without my hearing aids, the day seems so still,
light washes the windows all yellow
like the eye of my cat who snoozes on his wicker chair.

Yesterday a friend showed me her new poem:
seven hares running around a jar or an urn
the way they might have done in ancient Greece.

Only last week, Roger's ashes sat on a bench
in the funeral home, in a stainless steel urn
and I thought he's too large to be contained there.

By which I meant the largeness was his spirit.
The wake a great sadness.
Someone who seemed to be me

was standing outside myself
watching me comfort his daughter,
his two sons, moving around in a mist.

Now the clock that leans on the shelf above the table
is telling its silent numbers to the room. O — two, three, four.
Drapes hang heavy with dust, I must launder them.

I just want to sleep and sleep more, then more.
What does this world mean anyway
so small in this endless universe?

On YouTube I listen to scientists,
the many who say there is no existence after.
Stephen Hawking says we are only computers.

Can I hope anyway? I've read and read again
the few letters I kept from the great many Roger sent me.
And stared at the photographs, trying to bring him back.

Seven hares running to what end, for what reason?
Seven yellow pairs of eyes at the window.
Seven stabbing shafts of midday light.

Glosa, Four Months after Your Death

after Pablo Neruda

Nobody is missing from the garden. Nobody is here:
only the green and black winter, the day
waking from sleep like a ghost,
a white phantom in cold garments.

Early November, leaves on the ground,
the migrating birds gone from the trees,
shrill jay in the maple, his unanswered call.
I am alone here among the littered fans
of the gingko, the hostas' dried stalks,
alone as if waiting for you to appear
from wherever you have gone,
but there is only the silence, a gray atmosphere.
Nobody is missing from the garden. Nobody is here.

Only my own thoughts accompany me,
only the unresponsive sky, its silence of clouds
always drifting northward with the wind, and one
by one, disappearing as though year after year
was passing in procession, each loss making way
for the next and the next.
The hours are sullen and chill.
I gather the fabric of my coat to my body,
knowing I am not only alone, but alone will stay.
Only the green and black winter, the day

stretching out across the fallen garden,
the same garden that comes night after night in dream,
as though the remnants of ruin were haunting me,
the Eden after the fall from grace,
all bramble and weed, so I understand
that what could be kept has been diminished,
that everything perfect already had been lost.

I hold on to life like a bitter promise that has some good in it
and walk here like a first woman as if waking, an innermost
waking from sleep like a ghost.

The year has turned gray and gold and is hung with webs.
Somehow I have become an old woman without meaning to.
These are the rickety days of little substance, the mind
gone blurry, the ears deafened, the damaged eye,
even the taste of lemons dull on my tongue.
Nothing anymore, not even my emotions, is intense.
I have given up waiting for you to come to me
in whatever form you might take. I have given up watching.
All drabbed down, I am full of your absence:
a white phantom in cold garments.

Sorrow

The green inside of a storm wave breaking
behind your eyes over and over again,
smashing its long self against the rocks
at the foot of the cliff, the quartz, feldspar,
and black mica you've been climbing which are
slippery because of the ocean's foam
washing over them and there are fissures
you must avoid or step widely over, being
careful not to fall from that dangerous place.

All Hallows

This last October day I walk into the burnished world,
copper and gold held by frost and a cold sun,
into light brilliant enough that my eyes half close
against it and then open again to let the splendor in.
Crisped leaves crackle underfoot
and overhead clouds make the sky a work of art,
their white/dark scrambling across the chaliced blue.
After a dark summer, these are the days when
I come alive again, feel tears in my eyes,
joy in my throat that wants to call out
to the world to hold on now, just now
at the end of harvest and before the snows come
like white sheep out of the long barns,
the lambs of spring and summer gone from the fields,
the cornstalks cut down, pumpkins and kale
all that is left of the waning harvest.
It is now that your death begins to ease
against the ongoingness of life,
its persistence beyond the walls I'd built
of solitude and grief. Your absence, a quieter urging
as if I might almost believe finally in the spirit —
although there is still no answer from you
when I ask for one. Tonight, it is said, the veil thins,
the dead may try for connection.
I will listen hard for you.
I am close to you even in these lightening
days when half-rotten apples pile under the trees,
last asters line the brook, and the double-face
of the sun seems to be a kind of promise.
Every new poem I write reaches toward you.

The Letters

When you appeared to me finally,
there was tiredness in your eyes,
from the pain probably,
though the tenderness was still there
as you looked at me.
I knew you were dead
but I had been waiting months
for you to come in some form or other.
We were in my old apartment in Keene,
the one I loved on the second floor
of the New Englander, only strangely
it was your apartment now.
We were sitting across from each other
at the gray formica table
and I was reading you the letters
you wrote to me after I'd moved away —
ten years of them I'd saved in
the blue plastic file box in the back closet.
We were enjoying sharing again
the memories, even the bad ones —
the pain, the doctors, but also
the closeness of our years together,
a shared dailiness of our lives.
God, I was so happy
that I could talk to you again.
But the landlord banged up the stairs
and, without knocking,
slammed the door open with his fist.
He yelled at you that the State
hadn't paid the rent, ordered you out.
He ruined everything and you sent me away
without even your letters for comfort.
But now, a second dream:
you appear walking in a line of the dead.

They all wear garments fashioned
of their own essence. You are swathed
in blue silk which flows out behind you
like ocean waves. You walk in the line
and do not speak to me. The waves bring you
in to me and take you away.

Here

In the cabins in the woods where fires are glowing
Where the line of horses walks slowly through the snowfall
In the bags of the poor who gather apples and onions from the food pantry
Where the parishioners gather on the hard pews to sing the old songs
In the days when the churches have gone dark and silent
In the cities with their flashing cabs and buses and glass and chrome.
In the cities with their briefcases and the homeless lying on the grates
In the villages where old men gather at the post office to gossip by the mailboxes
In the villages where in the evening the lights go on one by one like watchfires
In the sky above the sky above the sky to infinity to where all the answers lie hidden
In the brook's cold water running around the icy boulders like lengths of lace
Where the mothers hold their children back from the winds of the future
Where we brace ourselves against age and the dark
Where on the hard streets a boy falls to the ground bleeding
Where the hunters strap the deer to the roof of their car
Where the refugees gather in the tents they know as their only home
Where the ocean gathers the drowning like thrown-away flowers
When the letters come with our names on them and the word love
Where the raptor glides and dives and the rabbit screams in the field
In the eyes of the foxes as they run down the mountain barking
In the broken and the sane In the people coming in from the cold
In outrage and complaint In hope and forgiveness
Where the woman bends down before a death and grief falls over her
When you wake and the sun is rising or there is rain or snow
When the fires are finished burning and the smoke has dispersed
Where a song enters your mind or many songs and lifts your heart
Where hope and forgiveness Where love

January Nightfall

From what unearthly blessing comes this skittering of wind-blown snow
off mansard roofs next door, the whoosh of white that sifts with a sound
like shaken rice across the snow-heaped lawn?
I watch through the bedroom window as the slanted

afternoon light ignites the maples until they glow, then transmutes
as sky passes through lemon, mango, peach and melon.
Suddenly it goes dark, night pressing down too early.
In here, the old inherited clock on the shelf reads 4:00,

the outside thermometer reads ten below. I want to know
what I stand here praying toward, to feel something
return from that unreachable Where. Though there's no answer back,
blessed be these rooms and the brash wind's evensong beneath the door.

Let me be like my cat asleep upside-down on the comforter
who is unaware for now in his still hour.

Memory

after a photograph by Yako Ma

I remember
the absolute silence of the cherry blossoms
over the small emerald river in the countryside,
the quiet countryside somewhere in Japan.
And the way the emerald water also held
the milky white reflection of the sky
and the dark shadows the cherry trees cast there
where a single rowboat was pulled up parallel to the bank
as I sat a long way off in another country,
another century, looking down on the scene.

I think it must be morning there, the air moist on my arms,
the small path that runs along the river, empty
but waiting for someone, a monk perhaps,
to arrive in his orange robe —
a monk deep in a meditation walk,
and he doesn't know I am watching him
from my opposite and far edge of the world.
Yet here I am with all my senses open,
taking in his walk, the river, the rowboat,
and the cherry trees in blossom
such as I've never seen in my own life.
And wishing to go in that oarless rowboat
somewhere deeper into this quiet
that I can almost remember.
How gently flowing my mind feels now —
like the small river
or an unfolding cherry blossom.

Birthday Flowers at Seventy-Eight

for B.

The daughter of the village florist
brings them to my door. Twelve pink roses,
twelve tulips streaked pink and yellow,
mingled stems deep in a glass vase.
They brighten these dark apartment rooms.
The soft-edged sweetness of roses,
the nearly imperceptible
peppery scent of tulips.
They are a fence against sorrow.

Once they were hard bulbs
and seedlings with tiny thorns
planted in the earth,
dark soil nourishing them,
sun that poured over them like milk,
rains urging them upward,
the hands of the gardeners,
dirt-grimed and sturdy,
the hands of those others
whose hands have touched them.

I send thanks to my friend
with whom I share joy and grief.
A week from now,
the petals full-opened will fall
like torn pieces of tissue
or notes from a stave,
still beautiful on my rock-maple table.

Reincarnate

I want to come back as that ordinary
garden snail, carting my brown-striped spiral shell
onto the mushroom which has sprouted
after overnight rain so I can stretch
my tentacles toward the slightly drooping
and pimpled raspberry, sweet and pulsing —
a thumb that bends on its stalk from the crown
of small leaves, weighed down by the almost
translucent shining drop of dew I have
been reaching and reaching toward my whole life.

from Necessary Light (1999)

How This Poet Thinks

I don't think
like lawyers, quick in the mind,
rapid as a rat-a-tat-tat,
or academics, who pile logic up
like wood to get them through the winter.

I think the way someone listens
in a still place for the sound of quiet —
or the way my body sways
at the transition zone, back and forth
between field and woods — a witching stick —

or as though I were inhabiting the seasons
between winter and spring,
between summer and fall —
finding those in-between places
that need me to name them.

When I think, sometimes it is
like objects rushing through a tunnel,
and sometimes
it is like water in a well with dirt sides,
where the wetness is completely absorbed

and the ground rings with dampness,
becomes a changed thing.
Other times
it is the way sea fog rises off
the swelling green of the ocean
and covers everything but illuminates itself.

I think with my skin open like the frog
who takes in the rain by osmosis.
I delve into the groundhog holes

where no words follow.
Slow, so slow I think, and cannot hold
the thoughts except when they come down

hard on the paper where they are malleable,
can be shifted, worked at like clay.
I think like this: with my brain stem,
and with the site of emotions
the way I imagine the fox thinks,
trapped in his present need

but moving freely — his eyes quick
toward the day's desire —
and the way, beneath the surface
of the water, the swimmer's legs hang down
above the tendrils of the jelly fish
which wave in the filtered light.

I think in tortoise-time,
dream-time, limbic time,
like a waterfall, a moth's wing,
like snow — that soundless, that white.

Landscape in Blue and Bronze

If she had lived my mother would have told me
how my father wanted to hold her back from dying,
how he would if he could have, his arms
surrounding her all through her illness,

his hands, familiar as her own,
tracing the lines of her hips, the cord of spine —
wings brushing her inner thighs,
slow and insistent, committing her to memory.

She would have told how newborn
I burst from such touch, the way a conch shell
delivers itself from wave to sand, a life unspiraling.

Once in Guadeloupe I walked in the night
with a man from Majorca. He led me
out onto a dock that stretched into the Caribbean.

He didn't speak my language.
In silence we knelt
in the blue universe to watch fish shoaling,
their silver turned to bronze by the undersea pier lights.

Later in a white stucco room filled with music,
his hands were wings, his arms filled with light.
He showed me in most eloquent language
how love can be beautiful and brief — a fishtail
flashing away into darkness.

If my mother could return she would understand.
She would tell me all love is brief,
how memory can hold for a lifetime, how death

is like the sea where the fire-coral drops off
to bottomless canyon and bronze light deepens
to thickest blue and what waits there

is huge and tentacled — a reaching shadow.
She would tell me that nothing in the end
could have held her back
from swimming hard and fast away
toward the deepest water, its blue embrace.

Breaking Silence — For My Son

The night you were conceived
your father drove up Avon Mountain
and into the roadside rest stop
that looked over the little city,
its handful of scattered sparks.
I was eighteen and thin then
but the front seat of the 1956 Dodge
seemed cramped and dark,
the new diamond I hadn't known
how to refuse trapping flecks of light.
Even then the blackness was thick
as a muck you could swim through.
Your father pushed me down
on the scratchy seat, not roughly
but as if staking a claim,
and his face rose like
a thin-shadowed moon above me.
My legs ached in those peculiar angles,
my head bumped against the door.
I know you want me to say I loved him
but I wanted only to belong — to anyone.
So I let it happen,
the way I let all of it happen —
the marriage, his drinking, the rage.
This is not to say I loved you any less —
only I was young and didn't know yet
we can choose our lives.
It was dark in the car.
Such weight and pressure,
the wet earthy smell of night,
a slickness like glue.
And in a distant inviolate place,
as though it had nothing at all
to do with him, you were a spark
in silence catching.

Naming My Daughter

The one who took hold in the cold night
The one who kicked loudly
The one who slid down quickly in the ice storm
She who came while the doctor was eating dessert
New one held up by heels in the glare
The river between two brothers
Second pot on the stove
Princess of a hundred dolls
Hair like water falling beneath moonlight
Strides into the day
She who runs away with motorcycle club president
Daughter kicked with a boot
Daughter blizzard in the sky
Daughter night-pocket
She who sells sports club memberships
One who loves over and over
She who wants child but lost one
She who wants marriage but has none
She who never gives up
Diana (Goddess of the Chase)
Doris (for the carrot-top grandmother
she never knew)
Fargnoli (for the father
who drank and left and died)
Peter Pan, Iron Pumper
Tumbleweed who goes months without calling
Daughter who is a pillar of light
Daughter mirror. Daughter stands alone
Daughter boomerang who always comes back
Daughter who flies forward into the day
where I will be nameless.

From a Rented Cottage by Winnisquam in Rain

In the Lake Region Hospital
someone I love is in danger, could be dying.
And because there is nothing else to be done,
I keep watch by writing
before a window pasted with old seeds
as the gray lake swallows the gray rain.

It is early evening
and the lake is tarnished silver
in the gradual disappearance of light.
In the shadows behind me, his shirt
is flung on the chair back,
his toast crumbs still on the table.

The rain falls heavily from the eaves
like a song played over and over — a rhythm
that would slip anyone off to sleep.

Only I am not even tired
and I want the notes of the rain
to play like panpipes in the hidden places
where I think my soul lives.
I want them to take watery root there.

I believe I do have a soul —
else why, as I keep these long hours
alone before the dark glass,
do I begin to understand boundaries —

how near we all are to each other —
how near life is to death —
how near I am to rain —
how everything, sooner or later, crosses over.

He probably will be saved after all —
only something that's burst inside,
a small thing — non-essential and treatable.

And would you believe
that just now, beyond the window
and under the eaves,
in all the heavy downpouring —
in all the awful danger of drowning —
the smallest insect
darted up on its delicate gnat wings?

Evensong

It is dusk, Roger, and already you
are sleeping on the pillowback couch, head
back, mouth barely open, gray hair in tufts.

Across the courtyard, the windows lighting
have nothing to do with us, and I curl
in the old vinyl chair, watching you sleep

and watching the nightclouds roll in over
the thin margin of woods that surrounds us.
In this unguarded moment, the deep lines

of your face are as relaxed as rivers
that have wandered beyond their boundaries,
even the small, tight muscles of your eyes

and lips softened, as though in sleep you had
let go of your history: the pills you've
swallowed; all those admissions.

Dear one, the time I have feared the most
has nearly come, and I write this poem in
tenderness and longing for all I cannot change:

the way your illness slowly takes your mind,
what manner of living is left to you,
the shadowed space my arms encircle each night.

How I have wanted to take all of our
fears in my arms and run with you while we
still can, back to those years when your room was

one flight up in a house on River Road,
my poem was on your wall and beyond your
shaded window there was no world.

Lightning Spreads Out across the Water

It was already too late
when the swimmers began
to wade through the heavy
water toward shore,
the cloud's black greatcoat
flinging across the sun,
forked bolts blitzing
the blind ground,
splits and cracks
going their own easiest way,
and with them, the woman
in the purple tank suit,
the boy with the water-wings,
one body then another.
And this is nothing about God
but how Stone Pond turned
at the height of the day
to flashpoint and fire
stalking across the water,
climbing the beach
among the screams
and the odor of burned skin
until twelve of them
curled lifeless on sand
or floated on the tipped
white caps of the surface,
and twenty-two more
walked into the rest
of their lives
knowing what waits
in the clouds to claim them
is random —
that nothing can stop it,
that afterwards the pond
smooths to a stillness
that gives back,
as though nothing could move it,
the vacant imponderable sky.

Watching Light in the Field

It may be part water, part animal —
the light — the long flowing whole
of it, river-like, almost feline,
shedding night, moving silent
and inscrutable into the early morning,
drifting into the low fields,
gathering fullness, attaching itself
to thistle and sweetgrass,
the towering border trees,
inheriting their green wealth —
blooming as if this
were the only rightful occupation,
rising beyond itself, stretching out
to inhabit the whole landscape.
I think of illuminations, erasures,
how light informs us, is enough
to guide us. How too much
can cause blindness. I think of memory —
what is lost to us, what we desire.
By noon, nothing is exact,
everything diffused in the glare.
What cannot be seen intensifies:
rivulet of sweat across the cheekbone,
earthworm odor of soil and growing.
The field sways with confusion
of bird call, mewlings,
soft indecipherable mumblings.
But in the late afternoon, each stalk
and blade stands out so sharp and clear
I begin to know my place among them.
By sunset as it leaves —
gold-dusting the meadow-rue and hoary alyssum,
hauling its bronze cloak across the fences,
vaulting the triple-circumference
of hills — I am no longer lonely.

Winter Sky over Cheshire County, New Hampshire

You are all blue-bruise and magenta where clouds hunch
like shoulders above the mahogany tree-trunks.
Above them, you fly up, dove-gray for miles.
All day I've watched you transmute:
lemon, nativity blue, flesh of the broiled salmon.
All day you shapeshift: buffing-cloth, rock-field,
ocean roiling spit and spume.
I would paint you
if you could stop, stay pinned on the canvas
of my eye. But you
are a wily fellow — you leap up, the wind takes you, the turning
earth takes you. Oh you are breath of ginger, cardamom, peppermint.
You smooth my forehead with a dew-moistened glove; rub up
against my hips and thighs. You ring like a church bell,
clang two spoons together, bang pans and dance.
To keep you, I swallow you whole; my abdomen swells
with your thousand colors —
all my cells explode with your light.

Roofmen

Over my head, the roofmen are banging shingles into place
and over them the sky shines with a light that is
almost past autumn, and bright as copper foil.

In the end, I will have something to show for their hard labor —
unflappable shingles, dry ceilings, one more measure of things
held safely in a world where safety is impossible.

In another state, a friend tries to keep on living
though his arteries are clogged,
though the operation left a ten-inch scar

and, near his intestines, an aneurysm blossoms
like a deformed flower. His knees and feet
burn with constant pain.

We go on. I don't know how sometimes.
For a living, I listen eight hours a day to the voices
of the anxious and the sad. I watch their beautiful faces

for some sign that life is more than disaster —
it is always there, the spirit behind the suffering,
the small light that gathers the soul and holds it

beyond the sacrifices of the body. Necessary light.
I bend toward it and blow gently.
And those hammerers above me bend into the dailiness

of their labor, beneath concentric circles: a roof of sky,
beneath the roof of the universe,
beneath what vaults over it.

And don't those journeymen
hold a piece of the answer — the way they go on
laying one gray speckled square after another,

nailing each down, firmly, securely.

from *Necessary Light* / 59

from Duties of the Spirit (2005)

The Invitation

I have opened the doors
near the garden.
Why don't you come into
the unfolding
of Japanese fans?
The peacocks are strolling
among the lobelia
for no one but you
in this place where
the impossible
is shaking
its bright turquoise feathers.
I have turned
off the radio,
washed purple and green grapes
for the pedestal table,
filled frosted goblets
with fresh well water.
Afterwards the bed,
its turned-down silk.
What you have left behind
will forget you
soon enough.

First Night with Strangers

The bat veered erratically over us
on that first nervous night,
while we ate, the twelve of us, at long tables
in the three-sided shed behind the lodge
protected from the summer rain —
which was hammering straight down —
and the lightning.

A thing so dark, it seemed
snipped from the burlap of shadow
high in the rafters above our candlelight.
Something not real — a figment,
a frantic silhouette.
And all the while we
(who were not terribly disturbed)

continued to pass the good food,
continued to reach tentatively,
stranger to stranger. Oh
we were jovial — we told jokes,
we laughed, we cracked open the closed
doors of ourselves to each other.

And, for all that society, I
might have missed it entirely —
so far above us it fluttered.
Seen/unseen. Seen/unseen.

Happiness

The old couple sits on the stone ledge to the stucco house,
laughing, while the bells ring in the village.

There are stones embedded in the earth, and scant grass.
The wall of the house behind them is very old,
storm-stained, time-stained.

The sheep wander into the dooryard and eat the grass.
Did I say the house is very old? Yes,

and the stones embedded in the earth and the sheep
are old and the flowered house dress of the woman,
the dusty shoes of the man, the teeth the man is missing — all old.

This must be Italy, or maybe France, I'll never know.
But I know about age and laughter — even about missing teeth.

The woman's arm, which is wrinkled like linen, touches the man's.
Or his arm touches hers — it's hard to tell. She wears no ring.

And the man has one of those flat wool caps the Irish wear.
Maybe they are Irish and have lived through The Troubles.
Maybe they remember hunger.

And because they are old, I know people have died in their lives.
Friends with hearts that burned out, sons caught
in a crossfire — something like that.

There is history in this story. And the couple is embedded in it.
They know this, but they don't think about it.
The sheep don't know it, nor the grass.

Theirs is a young history, since we call
wherever they are "the old country"
and the couple is probably dead by now.

I'll bet they buried him in his absence of teeth
with his black horn-rimmed glasses,
and her next to him under a matching stone
in her scrubbed-thin dress, her blue socks, her sandals.
Bet they kept her watch on.

In Sorrento, widows come with buckets of water
and scrub brushes to wash the graves.
In another country, the villagers walk to the cemetery
after the evening meal to bring the ancestors
news of the day's catch.

I'd like to do something like that for these two.
I'd bring them bread. I'd ask them

do you remember the day of the photograph
or why you were happy?

I doubt they'd know —
happiness arrives for one moment
and then flees past the sheep, down the lane,

toward the village where the bells
are always ringing for someone.

The Undeniable Pressure of Existence

I saw the fox running by the side of the road
past the turned away brick faces of the condominiums
past the Citco gas station with its line of cars and trucks
and he ran, limping, gaunt, matted, dull-haired
past Jim's Pizza, past the Wash-O-Mat,
past the Thai Garden, his sides heaving like bellows
and he kept running to where the interstate
crossed the state road and he reached it and ran on
under the underpass and beyond it past the perfect
rows of split-levels, their identical driveways,
their brookless and forestless yards,
and from my moving car, I watched him,
helpless to do anything to help him, certain he was beyond
any aid, any desire to save him, and he ran loping on,
far out of his element, sick, panting, starving,
his eyes fixed on some point ahead of him, some fierce
invisible voice, some possible salvation
in all this hopelessness, that only he could see.

Fun

Of course when I think about fun,
I think of a man in a short buckskin skirt,
shirtless, walking down the street
of the Bridge of Flowers
with a crossbow, a quiver of arrows on his back.
About fifty, an ordinary man
I wouldn't have noticed
but for the crossbow and his half-nakedness —
in other words, his way of sticking out
in the crowd of tourists going by.
He was just walking; a man in a suit
walking beside him, both of them
with a sense of purpose,
both obviously on the way to somewhere.
The street slanted up a little and they bent forward
to accommodate it. This must have been
their mission that day — onward and upward.
The bow rattled on his back,
the arrows quivered.
His hair was white — if that helps.
The problem with such fun
is that nobody explains it. It enters stage left
and goes off stage right into the wings.
Then for years it keeps going off in your mind
like flashbulbs. It takes on weight, metaphor:
Father Death, Creative Spirit.
Gosh I wish I'd known the whole story —
I could put the puzzle to bed then —
if only I knew the meaning of it all.

Answers for the Scientists Who Have Wired the Heads of Zebra Finches to Study Their Dreams

They dream in song, of course, birds do: hundred songs
of the marsh wren, twenty of song sparrow, three hundred calls
of the crow, each bird naming itself in melody or hoot, rasp,

whistle, squawk, drumming. Such a Babel. No,
a concerto. Interval and time signature, staccato,
legato, tremolo, the retardando of evening.

They dream sounds we cannot hear,
things we cannot see or feel —
infrasounds, ultraviolet light, magnetic fields of the earth.

They dream the north and west of flowers, longitude
and latitude of home. This is what they sing
in their wide-eyed sleep: blueprints for the nest,

twigs woven in careful design, spider silk,
lump of cow dung, clay, all made strange by sleep's narcotic.
They dream dive down and scatter up, drift on thermal,

balance on bough, bank and turn. They dream the currents
of flyway, wind pattern, star pattern; they give new names
to the constellations — bug names, flower names.

With their faster hearts, faster lives
they sing ten notes to the one note we hear;
they dream also ten dreams to our one.

Ten times the dreamwork to undo the stress of storm,
sickness, attack of snake on the nest. Ten times
the beak-language and solos that rise

out of sub-song into fullness. With what intelligence,
what emotion (how can you not believe this!)
do they dream of us with our gangly bodies, our instruments

and books, our feeding tables and earnest eyes?
Or do they dream of us at all;
are we to them of such small consequence?

Arguing Life for Life

"arguing life for life even at your life's cost"
—Muriel Rukeyser

Today in my office someone wanted to die
and I said No.

I leaned from the soft back of my chair
toward him as he bent forward, his back rounded
over his lap, his face in his huge hands.

I was long past menopause, family gone,
he didn't know this.

And I said: No, because you can't do this
to your children, and No, because
you won't always feel this way.
I told him how time is aloe to the burn.

He said he had a loaded rifle beneath his bed.
He said he could turn his wheel toward the roadside gully.

I said No to this man before me,
and I could feel an energy rise from somewhere
deep in my body and cast out beyond me,
toward him — a hot energy — a river, a rope.
It wanted to pull him up.

He closed against it. He shut up like a cave-door
overgrown with tangled thorns.
He went somewhere else —
narrow passage, so dark and steep
I couldn't climb down.

I leaned back, let my hands fall;
both of us were tired of pain
and loss tallied week after week.

He didn't know how sometimes I stand
at my bedroom window looking out
where the white steeple lifts over the town,
wondering what is left to tether me to the earth.
We sat a long time in silence.

Pistachios

Take a simple thing like pistachios.
Think of them in their smooth brown cases
or cracked open to white meat shiny as a tooth.
Or think of them in ice cream, the green of mint
or spring or something more succulent,
an unnamable ecstasy.
Get into the nuttiness of them,
the unadorned goodness, then let the mind go
wherever it goes from there, to Romeo in the garden,
to the full brown nipples of Juliet. Let love
come into it
as the *raison d'être* for all Being,
and because
someone's always starting a war, let war come into it,
though you wish it wouldn't.
Missiles over a ragged country;
worn-out people not turning back
to watch their homes on fire.
And from there go
to guns in the streets of our own country
and murders in the parks where no one is safe,
to feeble attempts — pistols
that can be fired only by their owners —
as if that would be enough to stop the killing.
Oh, but Romeo
in the garden, in blue, and the moon over.
Oh, but Juliet on the balcony.
Oh, but the strong vine
that can hold a man climbing.
And pistachio ice cream,
a green you could die for.
And pistachios themselves,
the simple nourishment,
the hard welcome apple,
the fallen fruit.

Duties of the Spirit

"one of the duties of the spirit is joy, and another is serenity . . ."
—Thornton Wilder

If the first is joy —
the rhumba at sunrise,
a three-note whistle in the sugar maple —

and the second is serenity —
a chair by a quiet window,
the wind fading down the hill at sleep —

then the third must be grief —
rock-tight, then loosening like scarves the wind takes
across the ocean while on the shore
the shells' empty houses lie scattered.

And if the first is in the brief seconds
which are all we can keep of happiness —

and if the second waits alone in the hour
where the pond smoothes out, its surface
unbroken and the moon in it —

then the third which is grief comes again and again
longer and more than we wanted
or ever wished for

to wash us clean with its saltwater,
to empty our throats, and fill them
again with bloodroot song,

And if the first
duty of the spirit is leaping joy,
and the second
the slow stroll of serenity,

then grief, the third, comes bending on his walking stick,
holding a trowel to dig where the loves have gone,

and he weighs down your shoulders, ties a rawhide necklace
hung with a stone around your neck, and hangs on and on.
But the first is slippery joy.

Remaking *Les Deux Mulets*

after Chagall

I have cut away the bandit with the knife in his teeth
and now I can pretend the red on the chest of the mule
is not blood but blossom. I have cut away the bags of grain
that were lying on the mule's back, making of themselves a burden.
I have buried them behind the night. And now I can pretend
the second mule is only sleeping; I can pretend the night
pulses with dreaming, imagine extravagant music.
This is how I want to handle the trouble
in the world: fracture the sky into floating triangles, give it
not one moon but two, mount the changed earth
against a yellow background,
turn all the murders into sleeping peaceful bodies.

The Composer Says This Is How We Should Live Our Lives

He lifts his violin and gives us the fox
in Ireland running with wild abandon
along the cliff-edge above the wild Irish Sea

and I am back in Connemara where even
the pasture stones have names and the green
slopes are plentiful with stones and the sea-wind

where there are no trees to stop it rollicks
across the commonage and the sea is a wild rolling
and the composer's brown hair is whipping around

his young intense face as his arm jigs and swings
the bow across the strings and his body is swaying
and his shoulders are leaping and the music is leaping

and the fox is running with such joy along that cliff
red fox brilliant green pasture cerulean sky
and the wind and the white-capped

plum-blue ocean and a man's foot measuring time
in the sun that is beyond brilliant and the fox is leaping
forward along the cliff-edge.

The Leave-Taking

I wanted to be serene, without companions, rocking
      in the wooden garden swing,
only my own desires to answer,

no one who would go away from me,
      no one hanging up the telephone,
no one passing their fiery torch along my life.

When you walked out from the birch shadows
      where I had not seen you hiding,
and the flowers surrounded us, the mockingbirds

welcomed you with their multifarious voices,
      but you chose
to become one of them, taking leave from the hedges,

your wings broadening in flight, then disappearing
      over the fields beyond the gate.
I swept up dropped petals and held them

in the cup of my two palms, absorbing their velvet,
      their edgy fragrance,
before I uncurled my fingers, and let them fall.

from Then, Something (2009)

Wherever you are going

you will want to take with you the mud-rich scent
breaking through March frost, and lemons

sliced on a blue plate, their pinwheels of light
you will want to take strawberries you have stolen

from the farmer's night fields, and the sleepy child
you lifted from under the willow where she'd been playing

you will want to take the one-eyed horse that was never yours
and the obstinate cat that was, and the turtle with the cracked shell

you found crossing the hard road and could not save
you will want, especially, to bring with you the shifting

blue/black/grays of the lake shining beneath coins of silver
and all that lives deeper there beneath the mysteries of water

you will try to take a prayer you might have otherwise
left behind in case you need it — and a memory of the love

you have been calling back — but you will soon forget

when you go, you will leave the Giants cap you wore
to dinner behind for the others, you will leave dust

coating the books you meant to read, the books themselves
weighing down the shelves — it will be necessary to leave

the suitcases and tote bag in the overcrowded closet
and your two rooms for someone who wants them

more than you ever did, leave your tickets, and your Master Charge
with its sad balance — you won't be coming back regardless

of what you've always been told, therefore take nothing
take less than nothing and even less than that — remove your shoes

place your pulse on the table, release breath, leave behind the scars
on your finger, your thigh, the long one over your heart

Prepositions Toward a Definition of God

Beneath of course the sky,
in the sky itself,
over there among the beach plum hedges,

over the rain and the beyond and
beyond the beyond of,

under the suitcases of the heart,
from the back burners of the universe.

Here inside at the table, there outside the circus,
within the halls of absence,
across the hanging gardens of the wind,

between the marshland sedges, around the edges
of tall buildings going up
and short buildings coming down.

Of energy and intelligence,
of energy — and if not intelligence then what?

Ahead of the storm and the river, behind the storm and the river.
Prior to the beginning of dust, unto the end of fire.

Above the wheelbarrows and the chickens.
Underneath the fast heart of the sparrow,
on top of the slow heart of the ocean —

against the framework of all the holy books.
Despite the dogmas that rain down on the centuries.

Concerning the invisible, and unnamable power,
in spite of the terror

considering the spirit,
because of something in the body that wants to be lifted.

Because if not God, then what in place of

near the firebombed willow,
beneath the quilt that tosses the dead to the sky,

beside the still waters and the loud waters
and among the walking among?

The Phenomenology of Garbage

She is sitting there watching the garbage man
who pulled in as she was about to back out,
his green and white truck
blocking her way, so there's nothing to do
but watch as he climbs down from the cab
and goes around to the barn to haul out barrels.
Because every moment's
an occasion for attention,
she notices the name, *Cheshire Sanitation,*
and it makes her wonder what's being sanitized,
certainly not yesterday's turkey
along with the *Boston Globe*
and a popped volley ball
cranked down into the dark dragon maw
and smashed into some essence
of turkey/ball/*Globe,*
that makes her think of Zen,
how everything's connected.
And not the truck which smells like rotten pears,
and not the barrels, filthy, but emptied out
for now of what she doesn't want —
the never-ending excess.
And because she can't go anywhere,
she sits there (in her Toyota Corolla
with the rusty gash on its side)
as the grind
of the compactor drowns out
her dog singing in the barn, nose in the air,
and she wonders where all this stuff is going —
not to the dump, which is obvious,
but in the long run —
matter, not able to be created or destroyed —
the atoms of some long-gone Magna Carta

perhaps even now storming around in her blood,
kicking up her irritable bowel
or hurtling this precise minute
in the leftover turkey leg bone
down into the compactor —
Being brought forward
all the way from the Big Bang,
the whole mess collapsing
to no-time and all-time
the way everything's a paradox,
like her thoughts which are going
everywhere and nowhere . . .
which are at a dead end
and no end (so to speak), blocked
by this metal Magog rumbling before her.

Almost Ghazal with Thoughts Toward Spring

Nothing loosens the way a brook loosens from April banks,
ice hurls up along the edges, block after giant block.

Peepers rev up, mole salamanders breed in vernal pools.
It seems as if the voices of the songbirds all unlock.

A poet I knew lived in a mountain cave, wrote on trees
and sang to the wind. Light's time, his only clock.

Animals have souls also, and trees and blossoms, maybe rain.
Once I thought I saw a soul embedded in a rock.

The dream world is another as real as this. I pass between the two,
as through a membrane, through a line, or arc.

Winter leaves me in a hush, trailing its long scarf of hours. What door
slides back at last, Patricia? Light comes in. No need to knock.

Alternate Worlds

They are what fuel the dark, what lie
beyond the sheer curtains.
They are mysterious and hooded
like the woman in your dream, the hollow
before birth, what hides beneath the casket lid.

And this also: what whoops out
from the forest, the claws
of moles in their tunnels, the moon's
long fingers trailing across cheekbones,
the breath dispersed into ether.

You can see them from the corner of your eye,
hear them hum in the background of everything.
Or, on a summer night, a huge moth,
white-winged, full of grace,
darts across your path — and is gone.

Lullaby for the Woman Who Walks into the Sea

beginning and ending with halves of a line by Ilhan Berk

Take your nakedness to the sea
and lie down at the tide line while the tide is still out.
Lie down at the wrack-ridge where sand pipers skitter
over dried seaweed, your whole body exposed that way,
your whole spirit exposed as you lie waiting.

With your whole spirit exposed as you lie waiting,
remember all that has passed that led to this place.
Remember the tall fields of childhood —
how you nested in the small circumferences your body
hollowed out in hip-high grasses, how the sun filled
the circle of sky you could see from that perspective.

Only the circle of sky you could see from that perspective
was contained enough to blanket you with its comfort.
Sometimes small quick swallows transected the wholeness,
their flights, diameters. Beneath you, the shaken universe
of the insects went on without your knowing. Out of your own
shaken world, Orphan, you had escaped to lie there

as in this shaken world you have escaped to lie here
naked and waiting at the perimeter of the sea,
for the tide that will, in only hours it seems,
return and wash over you, its watery brine a balm
on your face, its foam spreading under you
lifting you like the mother you lost, her arms extended.

As it lifts you like a lost mother, your arms extended,
you will become a raft, bones rope-bound, wood buoyant,
and give in to the back and forth rolling of your own heartbeat
which keeps its watch over your body, which will become the sea,

which is, even now, beginning to be washed out, washed
into the waves and long sweep of wild waters.

Into the waves and the long sweep of wild waters,
you bequeath the many griefs that have entered your cells
and left their mark, the way algae, clogging a pond surface
with its heavy green layer, hides clear water. You bequeath the days
when your heart was a carousel of rise and fall.
You bequeath the reins. You let all you meant to control go.

The world you wanted to control and could not — you let it go
into the distances, into long sweep of wild waters.
You wait to be lifted by waves, mother-lightly, your arms extended,
away from the shaken world, Orphan, you have been wanting to escape,
all the sky you can see from that wide perspective will fall into the sea,
your whole spirit exposed as you lie here at tide line waiting —

willing your nakedness *to the darkening inswell of water.*

The Gifts of Linnaeus

after native New England plants named by Carl Linnaeus

What is sacrament if not to take in the names —
        the twinflower for instance he named for himself,
Linnaea Borealis, its fragile bells ringing

long past his brief moment in the world.
        Or smooth sumac for making ink, for spilling
on the page, for keeping what might be lost.

Not for me the altar rail or the intonations
        of the priest. Not the vessel lifted up,
nor the disc like a diatom on the tongue.

No, this is the body — this mountain laurel
        it is forbidden to pick, its blossoms like lights
against the dark woods, or the red mulberry

that failed to survive New England winters —
        someone's dream of silk that didn't come to pass.
And this is the body, the common milkweed's clouds

of blowing across the field and this, too,
        what is left behind — the dried husk. And this
is the body — lobelia whose name fills my mouth.

And this is blood — the wild grapes clinging
        to the wall behind which the traffic
of the interstate rushes with a river-sound —

and this too, high-bush blueberry whose bright
        gems gather a sheen of morning dew, their stain
on my willing tongue.

And here is New England aster, its flowers
        bluer than wine. Eat and drink, here, now,
on this giving earth, these sacraments.

On the Question of the Soul

It is not iron, nor does it have anything to do
with the fleshy heart. It does not quiver

like feathers, nor the arrow shot from the hunter's bow,
is not the deer that runs or falls in the snow.

It hunkers down in the invisible recesses
of the body — its closets, scrolled bureaus,
the ivory hardness of the chest,

or disperses through every cell. And also it flies
out beyond the body.

Someday watch smoke travel through the air.
Someday watch a stain spread out to no stain
in the ocean. The soul does that.

It doesn't care whether or not you believe in it.
It is unassailable and contradictory: the dog
that comes barking and wagging its tail.

It is not, I am certain, biology.
Not a cardinal or a heron, not even a thrush or wren,
but it might be a praying mantis.

It is the no color of rain
as it sweeps a field on an August morning
full of fences and wildflowers.

It is the shifting of light across the surface
of any lake, the shadows that move like muskrats
across a mountain whose shape mimics the clouds above it.

Weighed down by the vested interests
of the body it, nevertheless, bears us forward.

Easter Morning

Gray and cold, Christ rises again — or not.
Suits and lilies in the churches
where organ music ascends to wherever it goes.
The old woman in the upstairs apartment
has gone out garbed in red, her white hair neat
above her rounded back.
I am alone in here, as if waiting
with unbelief and belief.
Overnight the heat
has dropped too low. I turn it up.
Later, I'll go for lamb shank and sherry
with a neighbor. Lately, I've been worried
about death, how it will come too soon.
Part of me wants release
but we cling to life, most of us,
with passion — or not.
Hung in my window, a hummingbird,
blue and red stained glass, drinks
from a white flower. Life,
we sip at its nectar.
Yesterday, after my reading,
a man handed me two paragraphs
about his shaky spirituality, saying
mine had helped with his own,
and a widow my age claimed I'd changed her life.
Such praise, hard to let in, harder to let go.
What do they know
of me except what I've written?
And what has that to do with this
awkward woman fiddling with her fingers,
biting skin off her lips,
becoming reluctantly old?
I live slowly these days,

puddled, stagnant, longing for rest, but wanting
ridiculously to be a hero, a Gandhi
leading crowds in my long white robe.
A weather vane spins on the cupola
of the building across the way. It's the ordinary kind —
brass letters for the four winds, topped with a rooster.
An arrow points to all the directions
on this earth it is possible to be given.

Then, Something

The moose and his mate
            stood in the roadside marsh at dawn.
They moved the shallow sheet of water,
the smallest rustle,
               as if ghosts were passing.

Together they broke the surface,
            such precision in their knobby bodies —
Were they only figments in the unestablished light?
But something held them
             bound them to the earth.

On a rise, above them, just at the edge of the road
            in a kind of trance,
I stood, leaning toward them, and for a long time
we stood in each other's company.
             It was as if we were appearing

and disappearing in the dim light.
             The weight of shadow,
laden with gravity, shiftings, myths, a wild surrender.
We didn't move,
              but might have been moving together

through the shallow satin of water,
            losing ourselves, it seemed, in truth and beauty.
Or am I only making something of them they were not?
Weren't they only two moose in a swale,
              pulling up water plants, chewing them

just before full day fell over the earth?

Two Skeletons Found in a Barn Wall

One's arms around the other's middle,
delicate bones of the toes, the feet,
heads with their outsized eye sockets
in which I glimpse only shadow.

It must have been terrible, those last hours
in that darkest of places,
thirst setting in. Then hunger.
Only each other for companion.

Small inhabitants of this earth,
I don't know what I believe
or don't believe, but I wish for you
what I'd wish for my own:

may you have found whatever solace
you needed from each other,
may you have found whatever heaven
is possible and awaits your kind.

Late Snow

The light's unbearable.
What was frozen melts again —

the waterfall of water falls and falls.
This late snow's been nothing but a lamb

upon whose woolly head Spring breaks
into the broken world, o bright, o bright.

from Winter (2013)

Hunger

It is the gnawing within the silence
of the deep body which is like
the pool a waterfall replenishes
but can never fill.
The watery room of the body
and its voices who call and call
wanting something more, always more.

Once in a dream, the trees in a peach orchard
called out saying: Here, this bright fruit,
hold its roundness in your palm,
and I held one, wanting
the others I could not hold,
as the light fell through the trees,
one cascade after another.

Now, the wind from the hurricane
that veered out to sea
and the hard rain blow through the space
where yesterday men felled the spruce,
its height and beauty, for no good reason.
Where it was, only emptiness remains,
and the stump level with the ground.

The wind finds its own place
and waits there holding its breath
for a moment, calling to no one,
surprising us by its stillness,
surprising even the rain which comes in
to my house through the untidy gardens
where it has been sending its life breath
over the dying mint and blood-red daylilies.

Summer is dying and I grow closer
to the shadow moving toward me
like the small spiders
that inhabit and hunt in the corners.
And the wind stirs, rattles the panels
singing its own hunger, its own water song.

Winter Grace

If you have seen the snow
under the lamppost
piled up like a white beaver hat on the picnic table
or somewhere slowly falling
into the brook
to be swallowed by water,
then you have seen beauty
and know it for its transience.
And if you have gone out in the snow
for only the pleasure
of walking barely protected
from the galaxies,
the flakes settling on your parka
like the dust from just-born stars,
the cold waking you
as if from long sleeping,
then you can understand
how, more often than not,
truth is found in silence,
how the natural world comes to you
if you go out to meet it,
its icy ditches filled with dead weeds,
its vacant birdhouses, and dens
full of the sleeping.
But this is the slowed down season
held fast by darkness
and if no one comes to keep you company
then keep watch over your own solitude.
In that stillness, you will learn
with your whole body
the significance of cold
and the night,
which is otherwise always eluding you.

Biography from Seventy-Four

Once she knew a blind woman
who told her
the dreams of the blind
are full of voices and sound,
the touch of skin on skin —
velvet and satin,
footsteps coming and going,
a hundred bird calls
and the well of darkness.
Her bedroom is small and closed in.
One window, a bureau,
a nightstand piled with books
and a lamp with bad wiring
that flits on and off.
Years ago in a bedroom
with a green light bulb
she spent many afternoons with a man.
Love is a house afire,
a truck full of apples,
a stream with shining water.
Here is a secret:
most days she sleeps
most of the day.
She is not who she was.
Last week, she dreamt
she could still run.
She ran and ran a long way.
She sleeps uneasily now,
waking and turning,
waking and turning.
If she could be anywhere
she'd be on the windjammer
sailing to Martinique,
the one she remembers

that comes back in dreams,
the sea dark blue and rolling,
that paradise, green mountain
and white sand in the distance.
Don't go back to sleep now.
Love is the sun going down.
She regrets not having been
a better mother.
When she was a child, her mother
sang her to sleep.
The last song always
good night ladies
I have to leave you now.
Her fine hair, a flame
wrapped around her head.
Her green eyes.
Suddenly, unannounced,
death comes.
Love, a map with no roads,
no boundaries,
wild and full of grace.
Grace: what is given
without being asked,
what makes one able to rise.
The last time she felt joy,
so long ago she can't remember.
She is afraid
of thunder that comes too close,
war and the threat of war.
She tries to protect herself —
from the wind of no good.
Her name means *noble.*
She's done the best she could.

The Guest

In the long July evenings,
the French woman,
who came to stay every summer
for two weeks at my aunt's inn,
would row my brother and me
out to the middle of the mile-wide lake
so that the three of us
would be surrounded by the wild
extravagance of reds that had transformed
both lake and sky into fire.
It was the summer after our mother died.
I remember the dipping sound of the oars
and the sweet music of our voices as she led us
in the songs she had taught us to love.
"Blue Moon." "Deep Purple."
We sang as she rowed, not ever wondering
where she came from or why she was alone,
happy that she was willing to row us
out into all that beauty.

Father Poem: a Collage

in memory of Edouard Henri Boudreau, 1906–1947

My father is driving Old Betsy down to Doylestown
from Hartford. Rain pours so hard it leaks
in around the door and soaks my Girl Scout oxfords.
Nothing beyond the windshield but rain
and the car slides crazy around the highway.
Somewhere out there is New York City,

far beyond it, the woman I've not yet met
who will become my stepmother.
The car lurches. I am scared to death.

     ❦

Winter, near Christmas. A light comes on
in the cold bedroom where I have been sleeping.

Someone has woken me because he can't wait for morning.
My father who has just returned has entered
the room alone. He pulls the doll from her hiding place

beneath his coat which smells of falling snow.
Her hair, dark braids, her dress shines in blue satin
as if she were made of stars.

     ❦

Why did you choose the Merchant's Hotel,
how long did you plan,
how did you get there?
What did the room look like,
did you call anyone,
had you asked for help,
was it day or night?
Where did you find the rope,

from what did you hang it,
did you stand on a chair?
What did you look like after?
Did you ever falter?
Wasn't I enough to keep you here?
Didn't you ever think of me?

❧

You were there and then missing.
The terror after which the body is torn
and the darkness enters it.

Dark night of your own dark soul, father,
  don't you still ride my spirit?
    Black horse, black horse galloping.

❧

My father arrives cradling bread in his arms.
A round loaf, warm,
and full of its own incense.

When he offers it, I take it from his hands and eat the mountain,
eat the garden of secrets. All the lamps of the village come on
as if they were voices out of time.

❧

On visitations, the way to somewhere else,
he'd stop off with me at the Hotel Bond,
mold smell of wallpaper, dust,
open whiskey bottle on the dresser.

Or at the PX, he'd sit at the bar
talking to the bartender
while I waited at a round table,
a glass of cola—
                                a long wait.
Or the Rosewood Restaurant,
where all the waitresses flirted with him.
Everyone knew his name.

                ❧

Emperor Penguin fathers sit on top of the nests.
Wolf fathers hold, feed, protect and play with their pups.
Dolphin fathers help in the care of the young.
The male bear sometimes kills and eats his young.

                ❧

I answered the phone and the operator said
call from Pennsylvania.

I was ten and I knew only one person
who would call from Pennsylvania.

Daddy I said and the man said who is this?
I said Daddy stop teasing the man said
is there an adult there?

                ❧

You won't undo what you did, you won't ever

be back

you knew this, you did it anyway.

But once —

at Riverside Park I rode a white horse
with a dark seed eye
and reins I held and the music played.
As you stood by,
the calliope played with a jangabell sound
"Til We Meet Again."

Father who will not be made small in me ever.

Old Man Wearing Vegetation

after a photograph by Rittai Konen and Karoline Hjorth

He stands in a salt marsh up to his knees in the black water.
Around him sedges and rushes grow waist high.
Over his shoulders he wears a long shawl of cord grass
which with one arm he clasps to his chest like armor.
He might be pledging allegiance
to the natural world he stands on.
Thinning brown hair plastered on his forehead.
Gray beard. Squint lines around his eyes.

❧

When I was a child I would go
into the fields behind our house and lie down
in tall timothy and sedges.
Hidden there, my body pressed a little circle
into the grass. All I could see
was the blue of sky above me
and those otherworldly beings the clouds
that were always trailing
across my vision to somewhere else
like a movie about almost nothing.

❧

The man of the marsh is not a god.
He has not stepped out of folklore,
is not part of a myth —
only an old man who has been talked into
standing here draped with what has been
pulled up from the marsh.
The photographer's vision. He
is transforming into landscape
the way at the end we all become
marsh grass, cumulous, sky.

Riding the Cog-Railway up Mount Washington

Mid-July, mid-way, fog closes in, the blue car rocks,
our bodies jostle back and forth.
You beside me, we are closed in
a world with strangers
riding at a thirty-seven degree angle, gravity pressing
our backs against the wooden slats.
The train, pushed by the engine, inches its way
upward toward the summit.
This is the only vacation we will ever take together,
the only time you have dared leave your doctors,
the cache of pills that keep
your mind on an even keel.
Beyond the windows, white and muted light
as we travel through clouds that are all we can see —
a wet gauze, ghostly wraps, the thin
blind milk covering a blind eye.
Around us the passengers stir, rustle,
a child cries.
You, who have always loved trains,
turn to me excited, whisper something,
but I can barely hear you over the racket
of wheels straining against the track
and the whoosh of the coal-fired engine.
The cold air gets colder. Rain
pounds against the car.
What is hidden out there: sheer drop-offs
to thousand-foot valleys?
Suddenly the engineer like some Norse god
in yellow oilcloth bursts through the door,
and the wind and the rain blast in with him.
The metal door, caught by the rush,
slam-clanks shut behind him.
Rain rolls off his slicker,
his wet face, his beard.

The air crackles: what message
of danger does he bring?
Wind yowls like a devil's child, the train clings
to tracks on a high trestle.
But he means only to tell us how far we've come,
how steep the incline, how far there is to go
to reach the summit.
I lean into your shoulder.
Against the elements we hold on.

Advice for the Sleeping Lady

Look at you. Again you have been sleeping
past night's end, shutting out the day
for which you have planned nothing.
Sleep, too much of it, your one great flaw.
Here's an idea: rise
from the three pillows and heated blanket,
and simply go
in your pink heart-printed pajamas
to the catacombs beneath Paris,
the Empire of the Dead.
So what if it's illegal.
A party waits there just for you.
Bring red wine and cheese for the cataphiles,
one chunk for the rat
that will certainly show, dragging its tail,
twitching its whiskers.
No one will know who you are
so be anybody, be Keats with his white hands,
Persephone hot for Hades, Eve
in a withering fig leaf that's about to fall.
Better yet go wearing a headlamp,
carrying a handwritten map,
and settle alone in a corner
in the narrow tunnel, near the moldy
stacks of bone. Settle into silence
deeper than any you've ever known.
A little scary isn't it, this death thing — a little morbid,
but sleep is brother to death the ancients told us.
You'll feel right at home.

I Cast a Net over Sullen Waters

I

To make a song, my hands tug at the bounty
raising the four corners.

A storm blows over the lake from Thunder Mountain,
the boats speeding back to the pine-edged shore.

Rain on the roof of the boathouse
and at my aunt's inn, a fireplace filled with fire.

These were the happiest days of childhood:
perch the chef pan-fried for breakfast,

the ruined rec hall, its candlepin lane, beside the field
of Indian paintbrush and white butterflies.

II

About my infanthood, I have only
a few notes in a pale blue book

about nurses and formula, my mother's anemia,
how I took a first step in the '39 hurricane,

across the second-floor apartment into a world
of my mother's applause and flood waters rising.

Beyond that innocence, in a far world, clouds
amassed in smoky rows

and dark birds scattered up
from the fields.

III

So many languages, so many intricacies of each language,
and how are we to understand each other?

There is a door behind which no one goes. There is the last
underground river and a boat that carries the dead,

until even the sea wants to carry away its own name.

IV

The stars cast their insufficient light
into the universe.

Comes passion, and the brutality I try to keep out —
blood and torture, the madness we do to each other, the earth.

V

The songs that continue to rise from our throats
begin again out of the fire,

out of the deaths and ghosts, out of the atrocities,
with acceptance, with denial or prayer — or with rage

so red-hot our hands shake from it, our throats dry out.
And still we begin again.

Shadow at Evening

After all day walking the Vermont craft fair in the sun
after the goat-milk soaps and rose-scented sachets
the bright pottery stalls and the wooden animals

while my shadow preceded me along the grassy aisles
and disappeared reappeared as I moved in and out
of the shadows of maples and gray ash trees

where the breathy music of the accordion player floated
where the field was vibrant with color and motion
stalls of candles relishes and pickles cotton candy in plastic sleeves

I drove home and my shadow rode beside me drove lazily
watching the Green Mountains pass outside the windows
home to my own small cache of solitude and grace

then my shadow disappeared into the brown carpet
disappeared into the bookshelves and the books
I never missed it but just continued on with my quiet life

but now through the east window evening approaches
but now night is knocking against the long shadows
of the street lamp as my shadow rises mysterious and compliant

and I beckon it to enter me until I am one with it at last
and I allow the day to close and dream to come
allow the dream to rise from nowhere and come to me.

Should the Fox Come Again to My Cabin in the Snow

Then, the winter will have fallen all in white

and the hill will be rising to the north,

the night also rising and leaving,

dawn light just coming in, the fire out.

Down the hill running will come that flame

among the dancing skeletons of the ash trees.

I will leave the door open for him.

Notes

"The Hours":
The epigraph for section II can be translated as ". . . and direct thou the works of our hands over us; yea, the work of our hands do thou direct."

"Glosa, Four Months after Your Death":
This is a response to Pablo Neruda's poem "The Egoist," as translated by William O'Daley.

"Naming My Daughter":
In the Yoruba tribe of Africa, children are named not only at birth but throughout their lives by their characteristics and the events that befall them.

"Duties of the Spirit":
The epigraph from Thornton Wilder is from a 1930 letter to Paul Stephenson.

"The Gifts of Linnaeus":
Botanist Carl Linnaeus lived from 1707 to 1778.

Acknowledgments

In addition to the poems published in previous books, new poems from this collection have been published in the following journals.

Cutthroat: "Dead Woman Sitting" and "Penitent Magdalene, Donatello"
Green Mountains Review: "Zugari"
Northern Woodlands: "Reincarnate"
One: "Fragmenting"
Paterson Literary Review: "To An Old Woman Standing in October Light"
Pirene's Fountain: "Eastern Dobsonfly"
Poet Lore: "Winter Day in New York City"
Prairie Schooner: "The Letters"
Red-headed Stepchild: "Water in the River"
Tiferet: "After Kansuke Yamamoto, from *Anxious Corridor* (1935)"
Valparaiso Poetry Review: "Hallows" and "Memory"

My gratitude to Jeffrey Levine, Jim Schley, and the staff of Tupelo Press for support and encouragement and for the beauty of their work.

And thank you to the following friends who've offered friendship, and/or helpful comments on many of these poems; Dorothy Anderson, Lana Hechtman Ayers, Roderick Bates, Pam Bernard, Wendy Carlisle, Scott Elder, Ann Fisher-Wirth, Ann Hostetler, Louisa Howerow, Tim Mayo, Mary Jo Moore, Brenda Nicholson, Alicia Ostriker, Susan Roney-O'Brien, Penelope Scambly-Schott, Barbara Taylor, Linda Warren, and Herb Yood. Also thanks to The Woodthrush Poets for their thirty-plus years of poems and friendship (Polly Brody, Susan King, Pit Pinegar, Geri Radacsi, Pat Ryiz, Carole Stasioski, and Jean Tupper).

A special thank you to Mary Oliver, who encouraged me to become a poet in the beginning and who has been my touchstone over the last twenty years.

And thank you to my children and grandchildren and great-grandchildren, whom I love very much and who have been anchors in my life.

Other Books from Tupelo Press

See our complete list at www.tupelopress.org